TWISTED YOGA

SeaStar Books
NEW YORK

by Pilobolus

Photographs by John Kane

Text
and
concept
© 2 0 0 2
by
Pilobolus, Inc.

Choreography
© 2002 by Robert
Barnett, Alison Chase,
Michael Tracy, and
Jonathan Wolken

P h o t o g r a p h s
© 2002 by John Kane

SeaStar Books
A division of North-South Books Inc.

First published in the United States by SeaStar Books,
a division of North-South Books Inc., New York.
Published simultaneously in Canada by North-South Books,
an imprint of Nord-Süd Verlag AG, Gossau Zurich, Switzerland.

Library of Congress Cataloging-in-Publication Data is available.
B o o k   d e s i g n   b y   E l l e n   F r i e d m a n

ISBN 1-58717-136-8 (trade binding)
1 3 5 7 9 HC 10 8 6 4 2

Printed in Hong Kong

For more information about our books, and the authors and artists
who create them, visit our web site: www.northsouth.com

The individuals in this book are professionals. The postures
presented here are not recommended for general use.

To the agony and
the ecstasy
of it all

Twisted Yoga.

At first glance, this may appear to be a new wrinkle in the ornate fabric

of mind-body synthesis. In fact, it is not. It isn't even really yoga. And just how

"twisted" is it? We've certainly been called a lot of things: zany, whimsical, lunatic,

bizarre, illogical, inane, witless, outrageous, loony, eerie, preposterous,

sheep-headed, birdbrained, and just plain nuts.

Well—maybe "twisted" says it all.

SITTING

SHIVA

Yin
YANG

x chromosoma

tout y

Bridge

of sighs

Reverse psychology

Wings of desire

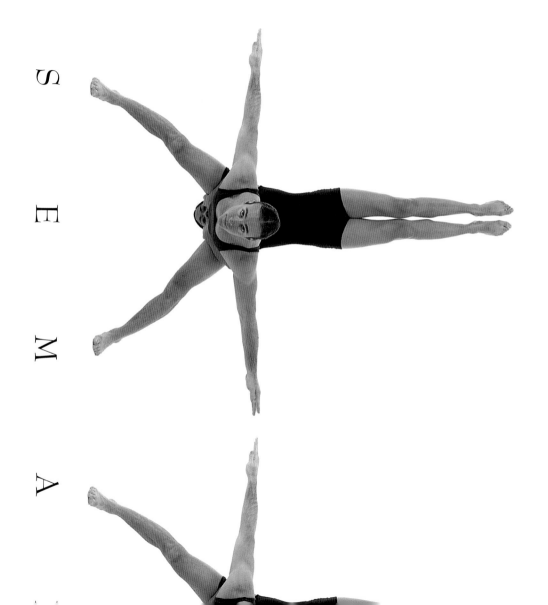

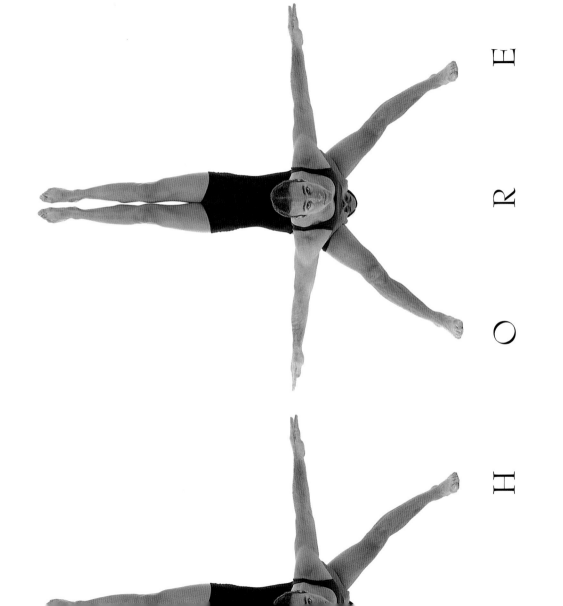

H O R E

MOON

IN

THE

BUCKET

Ante-cerebellum

The flying trapezius

spider's egg

NIMBUS

acute ANGLER

Nutcase

Bipolar

Bow di sattva

Mandala Mandala Mandala Mandala Mandala Mandala Mandala Mandala Mandala Mandala Mandala Mandala

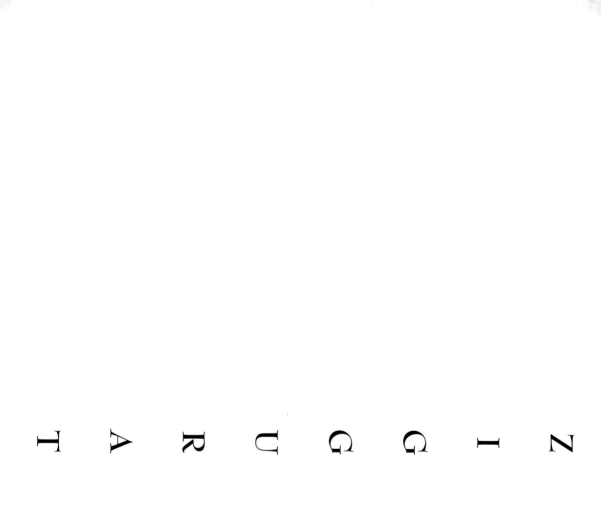

MANDIBLES

the gordian knot

The reflecting pool

BİCUSPİDS

LEGERDEMAIN

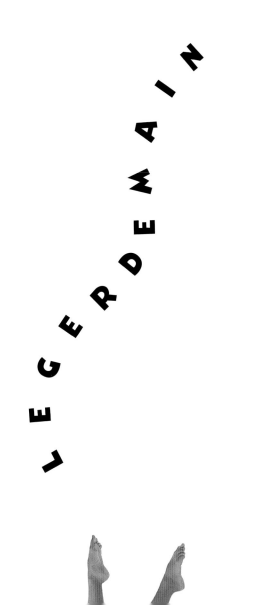

CHOP WOOD

CARRY WATER

FISHTAIL

Dichotomy

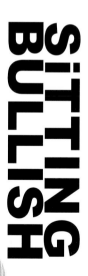

SiTTING BULLISH

SITTING BEARISH

H O M M E

HOMMELETTE

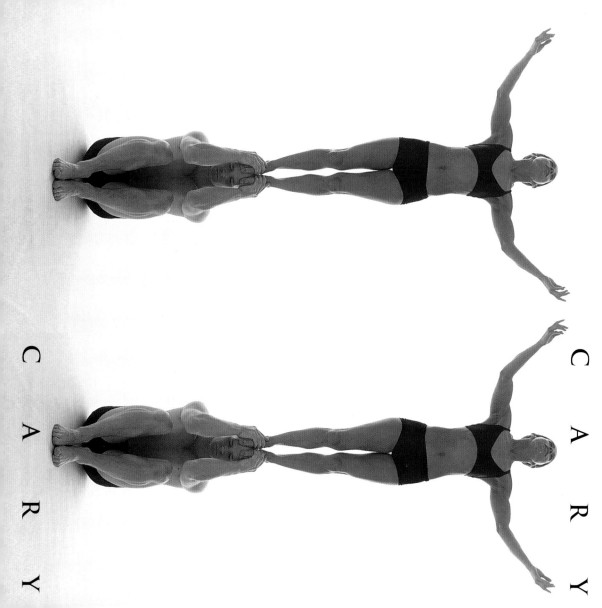

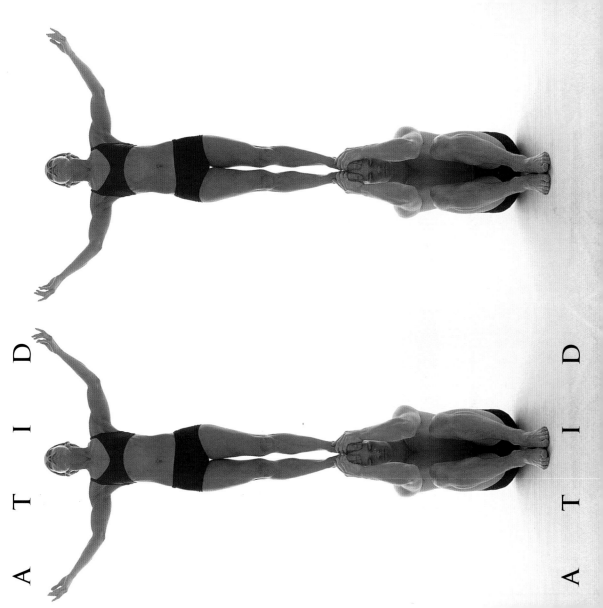

ee r z h c i r z s o

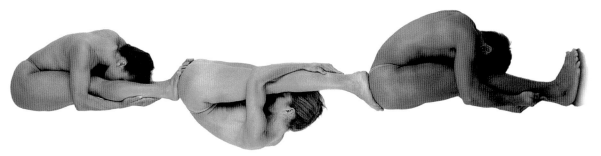

heart

chambered

Trillium

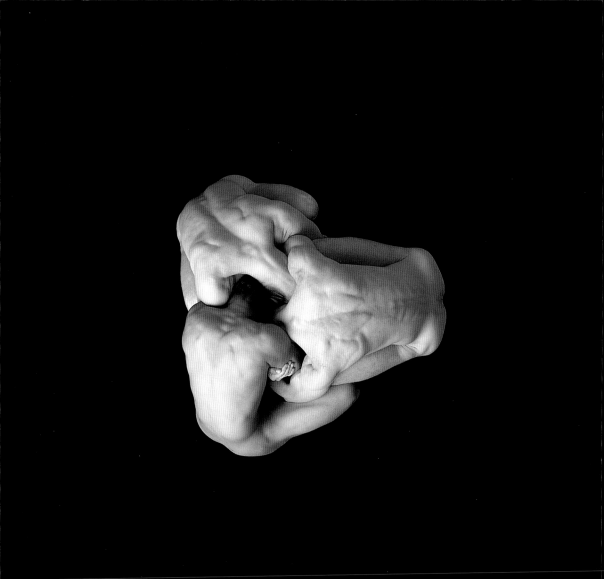

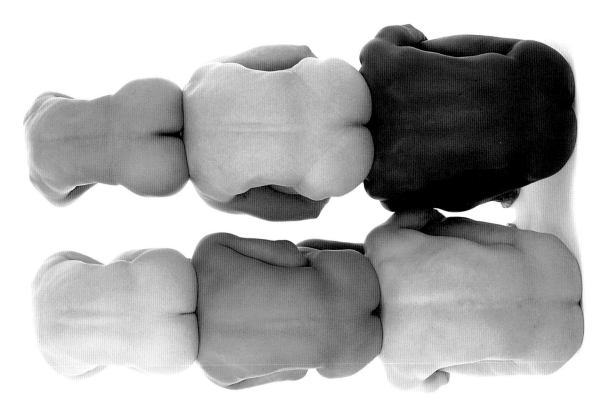

Pile o boli
Pile o boli
Pile o boli
Pile o boli
Pile o boli
Pile o boli
Pile o boli
Pile o boli
Pile o boli
Pile o boli

Laplanders

Acknowledgements

We'd like to thank our incredible dancers, without whose thoughtful and energetic output all this could not have happened: Rebecca Anderson, Adam Battelstein, Jennifer Binford, Otis Cook, Josie Coyoc, Renee Jaworski, Rebecca Jung, Matt Kent, Caroline Kinsolving, Gaspard Louis, Jennifer Macavinta, Emily Milam, Trebien Pollard, Benjamin Pring, and John-Mario Sevilla. Thank you, too, to John Kane, for the terrific photography. Your patience and good humor never flagged. And finally, we'd like to express our deep appreciation to the Joyce Theater and its staff for many years of emotional support and professional commitment to our particular vision of the world.

About Pilobolus

Pilobolus is a thirty-year-old major American dance company of international influence and renown. The company's innovative exploration of modern dance has given rise to "an art form of rare vision," according to the Chicago Sun-Times. In choreography Newsweek calls "as zany as the Marx Brothers, as clever as Houdini," the Piloboli transform their bodies into wondrous shapes with "stunning wit and physical ingenuity" (The New York Times). The Christian Science Monitor declared, "This is movement in its most glorious form."

Pilobolus performs for stage and television audiences around the world, and their works are also represented in the repertoires of other major dance companies. They have received several prestigious honors including a prime-time Emmy award for outstanding achievement in cultural programming. The Pilobolus Institute, an educational outreach program that uses the art of choreography as a model for creative thinking in any field, has produced major projects or residencies for the Lincoln Center Institute, the Juilliard School, Yale University, and the Cleveland School for the Arts, among many others.